The Psychology of the Politics of Differences between Men and Women

Psychological gender differences, gender politics and post-modernism, and free speech

Dr Marc F. Luxen

ISBN
2018 Marc Fokke Luxen

Contents

Table of Figures

Preface

You never acquired the Oxford manner... the ability to play gracefully with ideas.
Oscar Wilde

When clinical psychologist Jordan B. Peterson of the University of Toronto started a discussion about how we think and how we treat differences between men and women and sexual identity in our society, the attention he attracted was overwhelming. His YouTube channel with amateur videos of his lectures and debates, had within months over a million followers: https://www.youtube.com/user/JordanPetersonVideos. His book *12 Rules for Life: An Antidote to Chaos* https://www.amazon.com/12-Rules-Life-Antidote-Chaos/dp/0345816021 became a best-seller fast, with over a million copies sold, although this is mainly a self-help book written by Peterson as a clinical psychologist.

Clearly, Peterson hit a spot. It all started with legislation in Canada (Bill C-16) that possibly makes even talking about sex differences illegal, because it is regarded as "hate speech". It also forces people to use personal pronounces replacing sex-related pronouns such as he or she by them, ze or zir. His fame really sky rocketed when he did a hyper-confrontational interview on UK Channel 4 with Cathy Newman

<u>https://www.youtube.com/watch?v=aMcjxSThD54&t=</u>
<u>1388s</u>, about his refusal to use gender neutral words, power hierarchies, sex differences and the gender gap in pay. He succeeded in defending his position that went radically against the current thinking about these issues in a clear and calm way, while Cathy Newman got embarrassingly lost in her own words.

One of the biggest issues in the "Social Justice Warrior Movement", "Woke politics" or "Political Correctness" is what they regard as the largest "suppressed minority": women. They advocate not equality of *opportunity* but take it a step further: they want equality of *outcome*. The use of mandatory legal quota of percentages of women in certain positions for example is a way of ensuring equality of outcome. The rationale behind this starts with the dogma that men and women do not differ per definition in any way, or at least any relevant way. Any outcome that favours men is therefore per definition the result of societal injustice, which needs to be corrected at any cost. Discussion of this dogma is taboo.

A case in point is the mandatory word "gender" itself, instead of "sex". Originally, gender was a linguistic term to name words in languages that use different types of nouns, like German or French.

These were called masculine and feminine words, mainly because that is how our brains work, but the assignment of gender to words is mostly arbitrarily.

For instance, "vagina" is masculine in French: *Le vagin*. We also run into trouble in languages that have more than two categories, like German (and my native language Dutch) where there are three types of nouns: masculine, feminine and …neuter. What is feminine about a prostate (*die Prostata*), what is masculine about uterus (*der Uterus*) or neuter about a woman in German (*das Weib)* is anyone's guess. Anyway, the social sciences borrowed the term gender to refer to the more societal and environmental gender differences, while using "sex" to refer to the more biological sex differences. It is very telling that this last use has become taboo. All sex differences have become gender differences, a clear example of the suppressive construction of reality by linguistic measures. This is a very common tactic of so-called Post-modern ideology that is becoming more and more dominant in Western societies. I will turn to post-modernism later.

At this point I guess I need to disclose my own background and position. I was raised and educated in the Netherlands, a country that is high on gender equality and left-wing politics. My PhD in psychology was about personality psychology, the part of psychology that is about differences between people, like extraversion or intelligence, and evolutionary psychology, the study of the human mind using knowledge of our biological evolutionary past. Maybe an example of this might make this clearer to you. In our evolutionary past, men were hunters, while women were gatherers, and took the brunt of raising children. They did this as a group. One prediction about IQ you can make from this, is that women will be better with words and language, while men will be better with spatial information. Indeed, this is what we have known to be true for decades from hundreds if not thousands of empirical studies. But how does this difference develop, and what about differences within men and women? To answer this, I looked at the hormone testosterone. A very cool thing is that you can estimate the amount of testosterone a foetus is exposed to in the womb by comparing the finger lengths of the index finger and ring finger (it goes too far to explain why this is here). Indeed, women who had received more testosterone than average scored high on spatial intelligence and low on verbal intelligence, and men who received less testosterone then average scored low on spatial intelligence, but high on verbal intelligence. I will enter the intelligence debate later with you, for now this was just an example to make it clear to you where I come from.

My position is that there still is a lot of injustice regarding men and women in our society, but our policies should be based on scientific realities and discussion by free speech, and not dogmatic force.

And scientific reality is that there are systematic psychological differences between men and women, and they are well-understood and relevant too.

Introduction: what is the issue?

Some people argue that psychological differences between people and men and women have a biological base and explain things we see in our society. Other people, and this is most intellectuals, think that psychological differences between people and men and women have no biological base, and are just the result of the way we treat people and men and women. Note that we are talking here about psychological differences, because there is only debate about psychological differences, not physical differences between men and women. (conveniently forgetting that the brain IS body, and that to our best knowledge, our minds are the product of our brains, and not some ghostly, mystical entity, independent of body and matter!)

Differences between people and differences between men and women is a highly political discussion, where the "biological, Nature" position is seen as conservative and right wing, while the "society, Nurture" position is seen as progressive and left-wing. The reason for this is that biology is usually seen as something you cannot change, while societies you can change (in principle, or that is what politicians are selling at least) if the outcomes are not to your liking. It is much nicer to think we can give everyone high intelligence for instance if only we use the right measures, then to think that intelligence is something you are born with. But reality is not how we would like it to be, but simply what it is, revealed by careful scientific experiments. And we have enough data about this to present a clear picture.

However, things can get subtle and complicated. Let's take a sports example, because here nothing serious is at stake, and this makes it easier to think clearly. We usually accept that men and women have different bodies, and so we have no problem in differentiating between men and women in physical sports. We accept that we do not make men and women compete on a high level in say, running, because women simply would have no chance. There would be no competition, and that is what we came for after all. Now, and this is important, this is not to say EVERY man can outrun EVERY woman, of course. This difference is a difference of the average of the group (we will talk about this kind of differences and the "normal distribution" later in more detail). Many women outrun many men, but if you make the best of all women and men compete, women have no chance. Of course, you could argue that running competitions are not fair, and they are biased against women. And they are, no doubt about it. Neither are they fair for short people, smokers, blind people, and whatever group you can think off. In essence, that was the whole idea: it is a competition, so we like differences between people to lead to different outcomes (losing or winning).

That is why we do not say: running competitions are not fair, because women have no chance: let's rig the rules. For instance, we could give women a certain distance advantage. Or we could simply rule that say 50% of the prices go to women, no matter what (sounds familiar?). But because sport is a game, we can afford a better solution. We have men competing men, and women competing women. Is this sexist? You bet it is. You cannot get more sexist then this! Of course, this is not a solution when it is about real things: we cannot build a female and male society, and simply not let them interact.

But let's have a look at a sports competition of pure psychology: chess. Again, men vastly out-compete women in competitive chess. So much so, that there are competitions for men and women, otherwise there simply would be no women at a higher-level competition (there are now two women among the hundred best chess players in the world). Do men have better brains to play chess with? That is an extremely difficult question to answer, but in theory, with research, we *can* answer that question. You could try an experiment: take a large number of boys and girls, and give them just as much chess training, and see what happens. In reality we cannot do such an experiment because of practical and ethical reasons, of course: you would have to control that everyone boy and girl gets the same amount of training, no cheating by parents, and all should be in the same environment, eating the same food, getting the same education, the same amount of attention etc. etc. We can use knowledge we already have to make sense out of this huge difference between numbers of men and women. For instance, men score higher on spatial intelligence then women. What if people with high spatial intelligence are better at chess? (I have no idea if this is so, and if someone did the research. Google it). We can test that. We can speculate even more: what if the difference in chess ability between men and women is not only a matter of innate psychological ability, but simply of motivation: boys are much more competitive than girls, and that sure helps you when you need to play a lot of chess games. Or take it one step further: maybe boys are more encouraged to play competitive chess then girls, and this makes the difference.

Maybe all these explanations are true, or maybe none of them. Who knows? But we can talk about it, think about it, and research it. We do not say: the difference between men and women in the success of competitive chess is purely the result of male suppression and cannot be discussed. From now on, 50% of the chess champions have to be women, otherwise your competition is illegal. However, exactly that solution is something that is seen as a more and more an acceptable solution to problems much more important than a silly chess competition. And that is what this whole discussion is about.

A lot of research into differences between people and differences between men and women that is relevant to this important discussion has been already been done. You can only have a meaningful opinions and discussion about these matters if you know about the results of this research.

References

Bilalic, M., Smallbone, K., McLeod, P., & Gobet, F. (2009). Why are (the best) women so good at chess? Participation rates and gender differences in intellectual domains. *Proceedings of the Royal Society B, 276*, 1161–1165.

Post modernism and gender politics

Basically, you can use language in two ways when you discuss something. Either you use it to find out the truth, how things really are, or you use it to win an argument, and forget about the truth and reality. A scientist is concerned with reality, but a lawyer for instance is concerned with winning an argument.

These two positions have been at odds ever since ancient Greece. The idea of this science that you do experiments to see how reality works, and not depend on authorities (the motto of the Royal Society, the oldest scientific club in the world was, and still is, *Nullius in Verba,* take nobody's word for it).

However, philosophers were pointing out that it is not clear if we can know reality at all. This is abstract, but it is relevant, so follow me. The argument really boils down to the fact that our senses can fool us. Visual illusions are a great example. We see things that are not there or are different from how we see them. So, if we cannot trust our senses to "report" reality to us, how can we be sure of anything? This is what Descartes meant with his "I think therefore I am". You can doubt anything, but not the fact that there is a "you" thinking.

The problem is even bigger. Take colour. You probably know that light is electromagnetic waves. So where does colour come from? Wave length is all there is. Colour is an illusion we construct. If everyone was colour blind, colour would not exist. Colour is in our heads, not in reality! (Philosophers call colour a "quale", an experience that cannot be explained any further. You cannot explain the experience "red" to a colour-blind person. Pain is a quale. A tone is a quale. The smell of pepper is a quale.

Now, if you cannot know reality in the first place, you can argue that every everything is only language, only interpretation: if there is no reality to know, there is nothing "real". There is nothing "outside the text". There is just interpretation, and all interpretations are equally true and valid. This idea is called post-modernism, and it is very popular in intellectual circles.

The thinkers who developed post-modern thinking were Marxist. They used the idea that everything is interpretation to bring forward their political ideas. They said that because discussions are not about reality, they must be about power: words and ideas are used to supress certain groups. Originally, in Marxism, these groups were the working class, but in the seventies, this changed into women, gays, and ethnic minorities.

Post-modernism is obsessed with the concern about language supressing groups of people. Because of this, it is actively opposed to freedom of speech: if words are only about power abuse, words must be controlled. The control of words is for post-modernism far more important than freedom of speech.

All this must sound familiar. Western society today is obsessed with sex differences (which must be called "gender" differences, the power of words), sexual identity, and ethnic groups. To give an example, let me quote The Independent of May 28, 2018: "… *(bicycle paths) are too often perceived as simply a way of getting "middle-aged men cycling faster around the city", Will Norman acknowledged. He said he was considering setting diversity targets for London's cycling population to ensure progress was achieved.*"

Take a minute to really let this sink in. Someone in charge of bicycle paths makes group-identity politics a main priority. Not the safety of the roads, not to get more people on a bicycle, no, to get other groups of people than those ubiquitous white men on his bicycle paths. In my mind, Will Norman has lost the path.

Also, the right to not be offended is seen more and more as being more important than freedom of speech. Comedians making jokes, obvious jokes, are being prosecuted and even convicted. Even discussing differences between (groups of) people has become taboo. For instance, post-modern thinking postulates that when outcomes are different for men and women, say the presumed "gender pay gap", this is per definition a social injustice. Any discussion about differences between men and women that may contribute to these different outcomes is actively supressed.

Equality of opportunity is not enough; post-modern society demands equality of outcome. For instance, laws enforcing companies to hire equal numbers of men and women are numerous, without discussion about possible bad consequences for men, women and companies. Often, an analogy is made with between measures of gender equality and the emancipation movement of African-Americans (is that still the right term?) in the USA. "Corrective measures", like setting quota of women in certain positions are borrowed straight from this movement, for instance. There might be something in this, but the situation of women and African-Americans is not the same at all. I think we can all agree the differences in social positioning between white Americans and African-Americans for instance are mainly, if not purely, societal. This means you might actually be able to correct inequality by crude political measures like quota. But, like it or not, differences between men and women are not like that. Men and women have very different roles in life because of our evolutionary biology: because we are a sexually reproducing species and men and women have different roles in reproduction and we have very different bodies and minds. This is not just theoretical, the studies and data are in, and one of the main goals of this little book is to tell you about these results. This means borrowing measures from the emancipation movement for gender politics cannot be done without special considerations, or maybe not at all.

Men and women differ in cognitive abilities, personality, motivation and interests. Ignoring this fact and pushing for crude "corrective measures" will be very bad for men and women alike, and for our society. Supressing the discussion by posing taboos about gender difference this is even worse, because it destroys freedom of speech, the fuel on which our democracy runs.

Let's turn to some psychology now.

References

https://www.independent.co.uk/news/uk/home-news/cycling-london-uk-sadiq-khan-bikes-race-class-gender-a8367916.html

Hicks, S.E.J. (2004). *Explaining Postmodernism: Skepticism and Socialism from Rousseau to Foucault.* Scholargy Publishing.

Individual differences: Intelligence and Personality

When psychologists study stable differences between people, they talk about personality and intelligence. Differences in how much we like to talk, or how precise we are in what we do, or how nice we are, are all ways of doing or seeing things, of styles of behaviour. We usually call those things Personality. On the other hand, being "clever" is more an ability to do things with your mind than a style of behaviour. This why this individual difference has its own field: Intelligence. Now, never mind if you think there are many ways of being clever, we can agree on this I think: some people are cleverer than others. There are differences.

To be able to talk about differences in a sensible way, you need to understand how things IQ or Extraversion are distributed in a group of people, and how to think about differences between groups. Let's start with a physical example. If you would measure the body length of say 1000 people, and you want to know how tall people are on average, you add up all the scores, and divide them by the number of people: this is the familiar average. I am sure you are very familiar with this trick. It is just that: a handy trick, like all statistics are. The average is handy statistic, but it doesn't tell you something important: how big the differences between people really are. For instance, if everyone was between 1.75 and 1.85, the average length would be 1.80. But if everyone was between 0.90 and 2.70 the average would also be 1.80, but in these two cases, the two groups of people with the same average lengths would look in fact very different! If you would say; there is no difference between these two groups of people, because on average they are both 1.80, well, you miss important information!

What is missing is the *variation*. The variation in scores has its own statistic, like the average. It is called the variance. You can see the variance as the average spread around the mean (the statistical term for average). If you know the mean and the variance, you have a good idea how the scores of a group of people looks like.

Better still, you could draw a picture where you put length horizontally, and the number of people vertically. It looks like Figure 1:

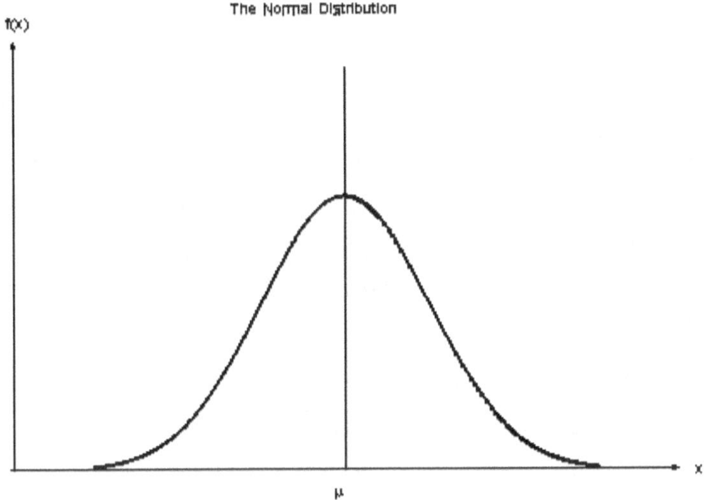

Figure 1 The normal distribution

(If you are wondering what the μ means, that is the Greek letter m, short for mean in a population. It looks intellectual).

When you think about it, this is logical. Most people are of average height, and the more extreme you get, the less people are there.

Now, the cool thing is, if measure things that vary naturally, you will nearly always end up with the same picture: a Bell Curve. If you would way cookies in a bag, you would get a bell curve. It you would count the number of leaves on trees, you get a bell curve. If you would compare school grades, you get a bell curve. Difference in intelligence between people? A bell curve. A bell curve shows the way scores are distributed. The bell curve is called the Normal

Distribution, because it is the normal way for things in nature to be distributed.

Hang on, almost there. If you tell someone how much the means of two distributions of scores (say the length of men and women) differ, you give them some information. But again, not much, because you are not telling us the variance. Let me show this in four pictures:

In Figure 2, men and women have the same variance, and a slightly different mean. That means they overlap quite a bit:

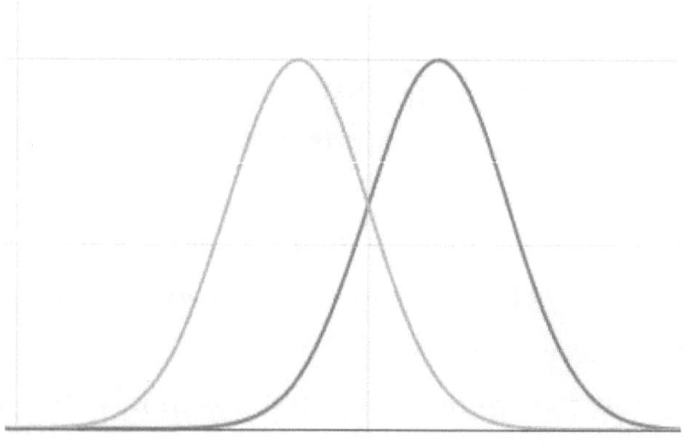

Figure 2 Two normal distributions with large overlap

Of course, if the mean of men and women would be more different, and the variance would be the same, there would be less overlap as in Figure 3:

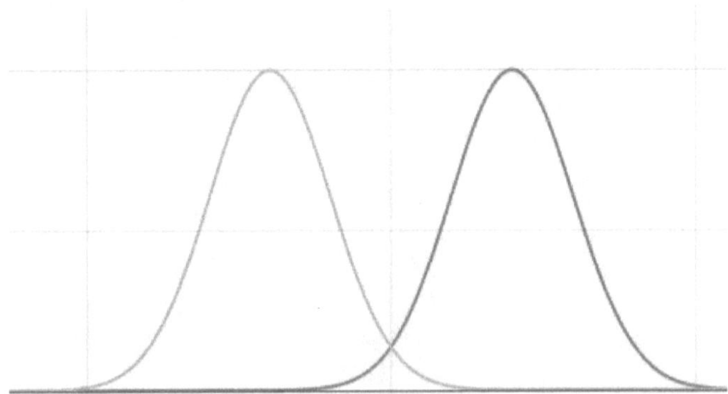

Figure 3 Two normal distributions with small overlap

But what happens if the variance changes? Well, if there is more variance, the overlap gets even bigger like in Figure 4::

Figure 4 Two normal distribution with a large variance and large overlap

And when the variances and the means are different, anything can happen, like this for instance in Figure 5:

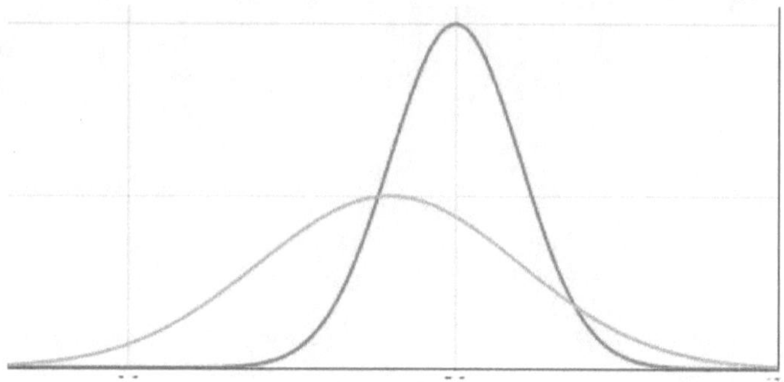

Figure 5 Two normal distributions with different means and different variances

So, we also need a way to talk about the amount of overlap, or more precisely, the amount of "shared variance". If two distributions share a lot of variance, you can predict one from the other quite well, if they share not much variance, you cannot predict that well at all. How well you can predict is expressed in a statistic called a Correlation (invented by the half-cousin of Charles Darwin, Francis Galton, by the way). You do not need to know how he juggled means and variances to get to a correlation, but you simply need to know this: a correlation is between minus 1 and plus 1. A correlation of minus 1 or plus 1 means I can perfectly predict one distribution from another, and a correlation of zero means I cannot predict at all. The rest is in between.

There, this is all statistics you need to know to follow debates on gender politics! Now, the correlation is probably the most useful statistic ever, and many people in research and finance do nothing more than correlation hunting. This is because it is very interesting and potentially profitable to be able to predict things. At financial markets knowing that you predict the price of oil, say from the price of iron in the Sahara (I am just making something up), could make you a lot of money, even if the correlation is only 0.1. Knowing that there is a correlation between how many steps people take on average per day and their chance of getting heart disease gives you a clue on how to prevent deaths. You could go on and on. One caveat: just because two things are correlated does not mean they cause each other. They just share variance, that is all. If you want to know what causes what, you need to get up from behind your desk, and do experiments.

Let's apply what we know now to differences between people.

Intelligence

Ok, please let all your ideas that you might have about intelligence and IQ tests go for a while. After you have read this, you can have them back if you still want them, no problem. But you need to know how intelligence is researched before you can agree or disagree with it any of the results.

Now, what would YOU do if you had to study differences in cleverness between people in a standard, fair and efficient way? Let's make that more urgent: you are not studying differences in cleverness because you are curious, but because you need it for real and important decisions. Let's say you are the head of a school, and you have noticed that some children learn how to read much quicker than others. If you put them all together, you waste the time of quick learners, frustrate the slow learners, and waste money and time. But it is not only about reading: you have noticed that the same children also learn more quickly how to calculate things. You have discovered that children differ in the speed that they learn.

You want to know who is who as soon as possible, so you can make groups and give them the attention they need without wasting time. (Of course, I could also use an example of a human resource manager allocating expensive trainings or putting people who can learn to do a difficult job quickly in that position, the examples are endless). So, you need to do something. You need to make a test.

I bet you would use questions. You would construct questionnaires with all kinds of questions you can think of, and that you suspect they have something to do with being clever, although you have no idea how. The more the better, the different the better: calculations, the meaning of words, making sentences, puzzles, rotate a die in your mind, common knowledge, whatever. And when you have made you test, you ask as many people as you can get your hands on to make that test. This is exactly what psychologists have done, we are talking about millions and millions of people here.

And now what? Well, now you want a way to see which of your questions work, and which questions do not. You want to see which questions group together, in the sense that people who make question A well, also tend to make question B well. But most of all, you want to know which set of questions predicts the best what you want to predict, whether that is school or job success. You are calculating correlations. First, you select questions that are correlated highly, because these measure the same (this is done by a technique called a Factor Analysis, but never mind that. If you want to know how this works, here an excellent explanation: https://core.ac.uk/download/pdf/27046866.pdf). The second step is now correlating the scores of the questions you selected, this time with the scores you wanted to predict (validity in psychometric speak). And you only keep the (sets of) questions that predict well. And, because you want everything to be fair, you only keep the questions that predict exactly as well for different groups of people, like men and women. If some questions predict better for men or for women, they are said to be *biased* and they are not used.

Now you can imagine if psychologists have been testing and refining since 1900 or so, there is a lot of information. They found some interesting things. One often-heard critic of using intelligence tests is that "intelligence tests are just one way to predict school or job success, and only a snapshot." Well, you can debate this, but the easiest way to say something about this is that are simply no better alternatives. Intelligence tests are by far the best predictors, and the least biased ones. Decades of research, correlating the scores of interviews, teacher impressions, colleague scoring, work samples, and whatever you can imagine we can use to predict the future success of people in all kinds of jobs and schooling have shown that IQ scores are by far, far the best predictors, and by far the most unbiased ones. And, since you happen to ask, the interview is the worst predictor (and the most used of course). This also should come not as a surprise: how can a subjective, non-standardised test like an interview compete with a test that has been designed carefully to measure just what it wants to measure?

Personality

Personality is a way people perceive and interact with the world which is stable and differs between people. If it is not stable, but changes quickly over time, you call it a mood. Moods come and go, triggered by the environment, but personality stays stable over time and environments.

By far the most successful and influential way of thinking about personality differences between people is the Five Factor Model, or simple, The Big Five. This time, unlike with intelligence, psychologists did not start by thinking questions up. They reasoned that all this information would be already available in the words we use to describe each other, so all they had to do is dig through the dictionary and asking thousands of people to score themselves and others, correlating the questions and find sets of questions that belonged together (Factor Analysis again) and that were good at predicting some criterion. They found five independent personality dimensions (factors):

1. Openness to experience;
2. Conscientiousness (being careful and hard-working);
3. Extraversion;
4. Agreeableness;
5. Neuroticism (or emotional stability).

(Easily remembered by OCEAN).

People high on Openness to experience are curious, and open to new ideas. They are creative, and they like to talk about ideas or aesthetics: they are often artists, inventors or entrepreneurs (or, sadly, unemployed), The prefer variety instead of routine, which quickly bores them. Here are some sample items used to measure this:

Positive key	*Negative key*
I have a vivid imagination.	I have difficulty understanding abstract ideas.
I have excellent ideas.	I am not interested in abstract ideas.
I am quick to understand things.	I do not have a good imagination.
I use difficult words.	
I spend time reflecting on things.	
I am full of ideas.	

People high on Conscientiousness have self-discipline, a sense of duty, and are sensitive to positive feedback from others on their achievement. They like plans. They are hard workers and feel that everybody should pull their weight. High conscientiousness is next to intelligence an important predictor of job success in most jobs, but not those where unpredictable circumstances are the norm.

Positive key	*Negative key*
I am always prepared.	I leave my belongings around.
I pay attention to details.	I make a mess of things.
I get chores done right away.	I often forget to put things back in their proper place.

I like order.   I shirk my duties.
I follow a schedule.
I am exacting in my
work.

People high on Extraversion enjoy interacting with people and are often perceived as full of energy. They are enthusiastic individuals who like action and having people around them. They like to be in the centre of attention, like to talk, tell jokes and assert themselves. Introverts need less stimulation than extraverts and appreciate being by themselves more. They are reserved in social situations and have lower energy levels.

Positive key	*Negative key*
Am the life of the party.	Don't talk a lot.
Feel comfortable around people.	Keep in the background.
Start conversations.	Have little to say.
Talk to a lot of different people at parties.	Don't like to draw attention to myself.
Don't mind being the centre of attention.	Am quiet around strangers.

People high on Agreeableness want to get along with others. They are kind, trustworthy, helpful, and willing to compromise their interests of the interests of others. Disagreeable people are more self-interested, and they will not shy away from a conflict to protect their own interests.

Positive key	*Negative key*
Am interested in people.	Am not really interested in others.
Sympathize with others' feelings.	Insult people.
Have a soft heart.	Am not interested in other people's problems.
Take time out for others.	Feel little concern for others.
Feel others' emotions.	
Make people feel at ease.	

People high on Neuroticism easily experience negative emotions, like depression, anger, and anxiety, they are vulnerable to stress, and see normal situations as threatening, and small problems as very difficult. Negative emotional reactions are usually long term, so they are often in a bad mood. People low on Neuroticism are emotionally stable, and do not have lasting negative feelings.

Positive key	*Negative key*
Am relaxed most of the time.	Get stressed out easily.
Seldom feel blue.	Worry about things.
	Am easily disturbed.
	Get upset easily.
	Change my mood a lot.
	Have frequent mood swings.

Get irritated easily.
Often feel blue.

Now let's be clear what we mean with personality "dimensions". Normally, when we think about people we think in *types*: she is a neurotic, he is an extravert etc. This means we describe a person by only one trait, and you either have it or not. But is not the way the dimensions of the Big Five work. They are not types, but dimensions, they are scales: you can a lot or a little, and everything in between. Moreover, you are not only on one dimension, but on all five. In short, everyone has a personality profile, for example like this in Figure 6:

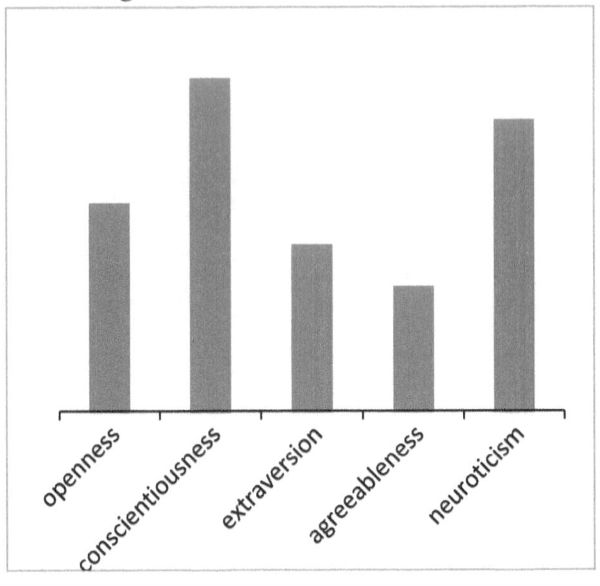

Figure 6 A Personality Profile as a bar chart

41

Or the same, but often also presented as a spider web as in Figure 7:

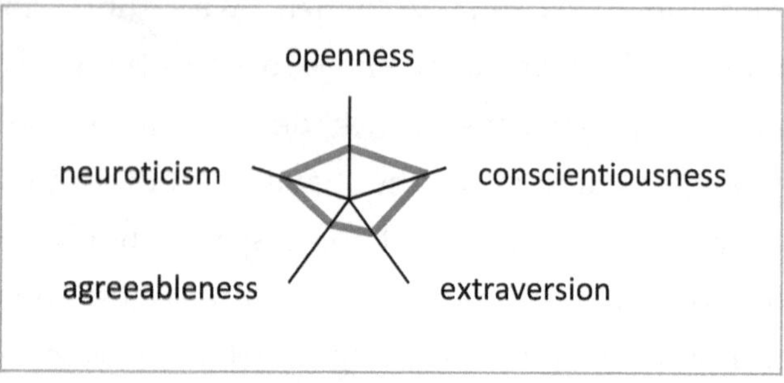

Figure 7 A Personality Profile as a spiderweb

So, now it is time to apply what we have learned about individual differences to psychological sex differences.

Psychological Sex Differences

Before we start talking about differences between men and women, remember that we are talking about differences in averages and variation of the normal distributions of men and women for a certain trait. Maybe it is good to have a look at this again in Figure 8.

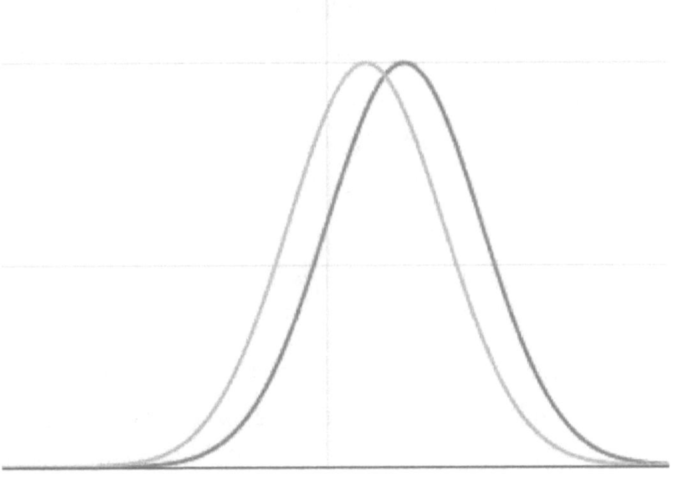

Figure 8 Hypothetical Normal Distributions of scores of men and women

Let us say that Figure 8 shows the hypothetical curves of the degree to which men and women are interested in people. The left dark curve is the women's curve, the light left curve is the men's curve. Although the difference in means are not that big, and there is considerable overlap, you can see that at the left tail (representing being extremely not interested in people) we find mainly men, and at the right tail (representing being extremely interested in people) we find mainly women. If you look at highly selective environments, like most high-end jobs and competitions are, people are selected at the end of the normal distribution: a small difference between groups has large consequences there, and you might end up with almost exclusively men or women. This is usually called a "tail effect", and I will show you real world examples of this in the section of gender differences in Intelligence.

It is important to keep this way of reasoning always in mind when we talk about differences between men and women (or any other groups, of course). In any discussion about group differences there is always one person remarking: "yes, well not all women/men" or "I know plenty of men/women who…). These remarks are true of course, but they are meaningless when you are talking about group differences. We are talking about differences in the means and variation in normal distributions, and the consequences of this when the environment or men and women select themselves, not about individuals you happen to know: "the plural of anecdote is not data".

There is a handy way to express a difference between two normal distribution with different means and different variances. If you don't want to read the small easy technical explanation that follows, just remember that this results again in coefficient like the correlation coefficient, where 0 mean no difference, and 1 or -1 means completely different. The trick is very simple: you "standardise" scores by first subtracting the mean and then dividing the result by the variance (or rather the standard deviation, but never mind that). This results in scores between -1 and 1. Then you calculate the difference between these standardised scores of men and women (always resulting again between -1 and 1), and you have a good measure of the size of the difference between men and women. To give you an idea: -1 or 1 is really an enormous difference, .08 is still very large, 0.5/0.4 is large, and around 0.1 is small but still a difference.

Intelligence

Men are better in spatial tasks and mathematics, and women are slightly better in verbal tasks, especially in producing language: writing and verbal reasoning. This is where we you would expect tail effects, and indeed, this is what we find on school tests and job choice. Wai and colleagues published a very interesting study that shows these tail effects clearly on SAT tests of 587,832; men and 585,518 women in the US. The SAT is a standardised test that is used in the US for college admission. Scores on the SAT range from on two 200 to 800-point in different sections.

Let's have a look at the mathematic scores of men and women. In Figure 9 you can see the proportion of men and women having a score of 200 to 800 on the SAT mathematics section in two time periods. A score of 1 means just as many men and women had this test score, and a 3 for instance means that 3 times as many men than women had that particular test score. You can a very clear tail effect: at the high end of the test scores there are more and more men, until at the maximum score of 800, which less than 0.01 candidates reach, there are six men for every woman.

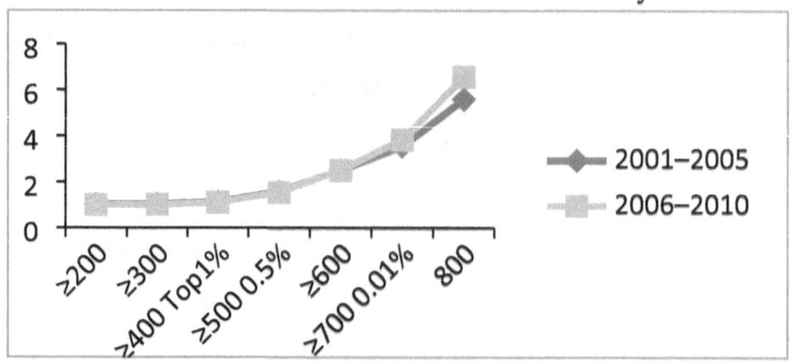

Figure 9 The proportion of men and women on different score levels of the SAT Mathematics for the periods 2001-2005 and 2006-2010

This same pattern is found on all sorts of tests of mathematical ability.

Let's now have a look at writing and verbal reasoning. Figure 10 shows the SAT writing and verbal reasoning scores. Wai and colleagues reported data for 2008, 2009 and 2010.

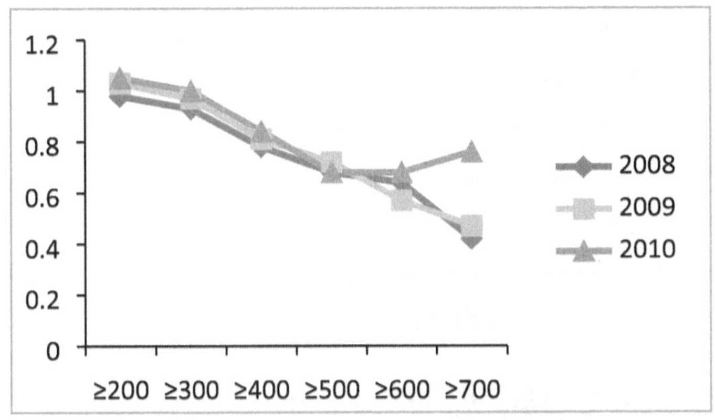

Figure 10 The proportion of men and women on different score levels of the SAT Writing and Verbal reasoning for the years 2008, 2009 and 2010

You can see that there are more women than men getting the highest scores, but the tail effect is not nearly as large as the male advantage at SAT mathematics.

So, we now have a clear picture of the most important psychological gender differences in Intelligence, let' s turn to personality.

References

Halpern, D.F. & LaMay, M.L. (2000). The Smarter Sex: A Critical Review of Sex Differences in Intelligence *Educational Psychology Review*, 12, 229.

Johnson W, Carothers A, Deary IJ. (2008). Sex differences in variability in general intelligence: a new look at the old question. *Perspectives in Psychological Science*, 3, 518–531

Voyer, D., Voyer, S., & Bryden, M. P. (1995). Magnitude of sex differences in spatial abilities: A meta-analysis and consideration of critical variables. *Psychological Bulletin*, 117(2), 250-270.

Wai, J., Cacchio M., Putallaz, M., Makel. M.C (2010) Sex differences in the right tail of cognitive abilities: A 30 year examination. *Intelligence*, 38, 412–423

Personality: The Big Five

Just as reminder: we are talking about Openness to Experience, Conscientiousness, Extraversion, Agreeableness and Neuroticism (or Emotional Stability). The data I use are based on the influential and large scale by Costa and his colleagues, who did a study into the gender differences in 26 cultures with more than 23.000 respondents who filled out large Big Five self-report questionnaires. These are roughly equivalent to findings of other, smaller and more specialised studies.

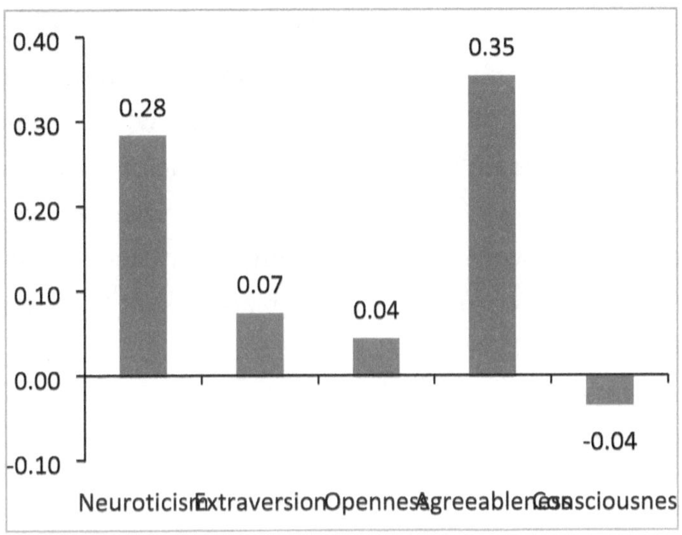

Figure 11 Difference scores men-women on the Big Five dimensions

The difference scores are shown in Figure 11. The biggest differences between men and women is in Agreeableness. Women are more agreeable than men, that is, women tend to avoid conflict and act in the interest of others than men do. The difference score is about 0.35. The next largest difference between men and women in personality is in Neuroticism: women are more neurotic than men: women are less emotionally stable and more prone to experience negative emotions. The difference score is 0.28, which is quite large.

Actually, the picture is more refined, with even more clear differences. This is because the Big Five dimensions are subdivided into different sub-dimensions (called facets). For instance, Neuroticism is subdivided into Anxiety, Angry Hostility, Depression, Self-Consciousness, Impulsiveness and Vulnerability. If you are wondering, where these came from, again they were found by Factor Analysis. Figure 12 shows the full picture of difference between man and women on the Big Five personality dimensions in full detail (data are taken from the study by Costa et al.).

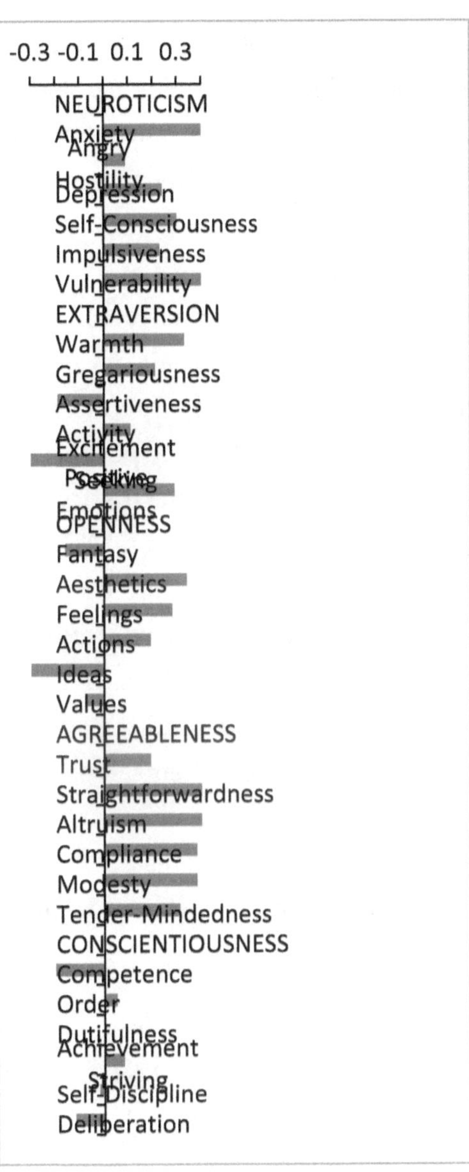

Figure 12 Difference scores men-women on all Big Five facets

On all aspects of Neuroticism, women score much higher than men. The same is true for Agreeableness. Women also score higher on the social aspects of Extraversion: Warmth, Gregariousness (being talkative) Positive Emotions (in the sense of experience being in the company of other people) and Activity, while men score higher on those aspects of Extraversion that are not social: Assertiveness and Excitement Seeking. On the Openness dimension, women score higher on those aspects having to do with internal experiences, Aesthetics (like arts), Feelings (experience feelings intensely) and Actions (prefer variety over routine), while men score higher on aspects having to do with external experiences and ideas, Fantasy, Ideas and Values. Finally, on the Consciousness dimension we find the smallest gender differences: men consider themselves to be more competent than women.

In sum: women are more interested in other people and feelings, while men are more interested in things and ideas.

References

Costa, P.T., Terracciano, A., & McCrae, R.R. (2001). Gender differences in personality traits across cultures: robust and surprising findings. *Journal of Personality and Social Psychology*. 81, 322-331.

Schmitt, D. P., A., Voracek, M., & Allik, J. (2008). Why can't a man be more like a woman? Sex differences in

Big Five personality traits across 55 cultures. *Journal of Personality and Social Psychology*, 94(1), 168-182.
Weisberg, Y. J., DeYoung, C. G., & Hirsh, J. B. (2011). Gender Differences in Personality across the Ten Aspects of the Big Five. *Frontiers in Psychology*, 2, 178.

Motivation and Ambition

The results on gender difference in Intelligence and Personality so far make perfect sense from a perspective of the different roles men and women have in reproduction. Women are more focused on other people: women are more agreeable and better at language than men, while men are more focused on things, ideas and experiences. The abilities of men and women match their preferences in terms of personalities.

Let's look now at a higher level at gender differences that has implications for gender politics: Motivation and Ambition. A recent overview in 2015 by Gino and colleagues showed that men are more likely than women to show dominant or aggressive behaviour, start negotiations, and select competitive environments. Men pay more attention to cues of power and are more motivated by power. Gino went on to confirm these conclusions in a series of nine studies using executives in high-power positions, recent graduates of atop MBA program, undergraduate students, and online panels of working adults with in total more than 4,000 participants, with the expected results: women had more diverse life goals than men, found power less interesting, associated more negative consequences with occupying high-powered positions. Women were also less likely to use opportunities for career advancement, but interestingly, viewed their chances to get into a high-level equal to those of men, but found this less desirable.

Again, these gender differences are systematic, and easy to understand from an evolutionary perspective of having different role in reproduction.

References

Gino F., Wilmuth C.A., & Brooks A.W. (2015). Compared to men, women view professional advancement as equally attainable, but less desirable. *Procedures of the National Academy of Science of the U.S.A*, 112, 12354-9.

Evolutionary psychology

As the name implies, evolutionary psychology uses the knowledge that we, our brains and minds, are the product of evolution. We are solutions to the problem of surviving to reproduce in the environment in which we evolved. Using this perspective, certain abilities, behaviours and preferences start to make sense in a functional way: they helped us survive and reproduce long ago. They were adaptive, they adapted us to our environment. Because most of us live in a very different environment now, these adaptations may not work anymore, or even will have bad consequences. For instance, if you live in environment where food is scarce (which we did 99.999% of the time), it is very good to like fat and sweet food, because they contain a lot of calories. Needless to say, these same preferences are almost lethal in an environment where there these foods are abundant, especially when the food industry exploits these evolved preferences ruthlessly.

Of course, it makes perfect sense to study human behaviour this way, because it gives you more information than just studying ourselves as if we suddenly dropped out of space. For instance, to go back again to our preference for fat and sweet foods, any claims that the food industry invented these preferences, but they could have been something different as well, become very unlikely in the light of evolutionary psychology.

To give it slightly more philosophical touch: fat and sweet "are" not delicious by themselves, it is our brain that constructs this experience. The deliciousness of sweet (or even the experience sweet) is not part of reality but exists only in our minds. In turn, this is the consequence of how our brains are constructed by our genes, and they have constructed our brains this way because it was adaptive: it helped us to survive and reproduce in the environment where we evolved.

Evolution works on selection, but most people only think about survival here. We call selection by the environment, so whether you survive or not, natural selection. But you may have noticed that I talked about survival to *reproduce*. In an evolutionary sense, survival is secondary: if a life form reproduces before it dies, it doesn't get extinct. And in sexually reproducing species, like we are, men and women need to find and select each other to reproduce. This means that besides natural selection, there is also sexual selection.

The most famous example of sexual selection is the peacock's tail. When Charles Darwin was developing his theory of evolution, he wrote that the sight of peacock's tail made him nauseous. Why? Well, because you cannot explain why peacocks have such a clumsy tail that surely doesn't help survival, so you cannot explain it using natural selection. The clue to the solution lies in the observation, that only male peacocks have this exuberant tail. It is not made by natural selection, but by sexual selection. Female peacocks chose males having ever larger tails. Why? Well, that is not relevant here, but I can imagine you are curious. They chose big tails precisely because they were bad for survival, because they were costly, and they cannot be faked. Males who can afford to have these tails either had good genes and grew up in a good environment, so they are excellent mating material. Or, to say this more formally, females who chose these males had more surviving and reproducing offspring. Note this is not to say that female peacocks think: "look at that tail: excellent for offspring! Who knows if and how peacocks think? What you can say is that evolution built the female peacock's brain in such a way that she prefers mating with males with big tails. It is perfectly reasonable to say that she finds them sexy and turns her on; if that feeling is the same feeling as we humans have? Who knows, but some similarity is highly likely.

This example brings us to an important principle of sexual selection: men and women have different roles. This is because men and women invest differently in their offspring. Typically, and this is the case in humans as well, women invest far more in offspring, especially in the beginning: they are the ones who get pregnant and breastfeed (this last was not optional until very, very recent). And if you invest more, you are more careful in what you invest in. This all leads to the biological principle of: female choice, male competition. If women have the choice, men must compete.

Of course, women nowadays do not need to be picky, because they do not need to get pregnant if they do not want to. But that information is not yet encoded in our genes who construct our brains and preferences. That said, we are not machines, slave to our genes. There are non-picky women and picky men, but there is an overall large difference.

Now, women can select men on many features, and they can use different features on different occasions, but they all boil down ultimately to two things: the ability and willingness to invest in high-quality offspring. Again, before you start muttering that is not how women think at all, remember that evolution works with brains that make us prefer things. We are only aware of these preferences, not where they came from or what underlying evolutionary reason caused them to be this way. For instance, many women like muscular men, especially concerning upper body strength (gyms make good money on this). The evolutionary reason is obviously that muscular men could offer more protection in the environment where we evolved. But of course, no woman, well, let's be careful, very few women, if any, would consciously reason: hey look, a man with big shoulders and arms! He can protect me and our children from other males: let's sleep with him! Of course not. Evolution works with the solution of preferences: she just finds him sexy. Or, to say this differently, sexy is not part of male muscles, just like delicious is not part of sweet food. They are all experiences just in our minds, functional because they trigger behaviour that was adaptive.

One very clever trick that females of many, almost all sexually reproducing species use, is to outsource the trouble of selecting the right males by simply using the results of male competition. They use the rule: let the males compete, and just mate with the winner. This results in a status hierarchy, where the winner pretty much takes all: the best territory, the best food, and most females. How pronounced this hierarchy is differs between species, and an interesting observation is that the more pronounced it is, the bigger the difference in body size between men and women are, and the larger the harems are of the dominant male. Think about sea lions for instance. But no matter how pronounced the status hierarchy is, it is always there. It is deeply ingrained into our systems, and closely related to hormones such as testosterone.

Now, dear reader, I realise that this was a lot of information to swallow, and moreover, information from a very different perspective from which we usually live in. But there is nothing controversial here (unless your beliefs overrule your ability to perceive reality, in that case you are beyond reach): of course, we did not come from outer space, and so of course our evolutionary past shaped us. However, importantly, I am not saying we cannot change anything because it is biology. This is nonsense. We can and have changed a lot: we beat most infectious diseases, invented glasses, and use dentists to beat biological threats, for instance. Neither do I say that because it is biological it means it is right. What is right and what is wrong is up to us to decide. But it is silly not to be informed of our evolutionary past, especially when we are talking about sex differences. It is even sillier to just declare that there are no sex differences at all, against all facts. There are sex differences, they are systematic, we understand the system, and they matter.

Nature and nurture: how determined is nature, how flexible is culture?

So far, I have shown you the results of research into psychological gender differences that are most relevant to gender politics. I have also made the point that these differences are not random, but that they are systematic. What I have not addressed is the question of the causes of these differences. The fact that differences between men and women fit nicely into an evolutionary framework of different roles in reproduction hints that these differences have at least some basis in our biology. Let's explore this question a bit further.

If you ask why an animal or a human animal does something, you can answer that question roughly in four ways. Let's take a human sexual example, because that is always most interesting to use. "A man sees a woman with conspicuous breasts in a bar. He makes eye contact." We can finish here. We now want to explain why the man-made eye-contact. The first answer is purely here-and-now-environmental: the breasts. In psychology jargon you can say that the environmental stimulus (breasts) triggered the behaviour (making eye contact). If you object to the sexual example, you can replace it by seeing a baby smile and start talking to it, or seeing a snake and run away, or anything you like. Stimulus-response. Most of us stop here thinking about causes, because these are obvious. But there are three other, let's say deeper or more distant explanations you need to consider. The first more distant answer is "the man's brain has been constructed in such a way that he gets motivated by swellings on a female chest to make contact". The next even more distant answer is that such and such genes together with such and such development build a brain that finds swellings on a female chest etc. And the last most distant answer is an evolutionary answer: what is the function in terms of survival and reproduction. This man gets motivated by swellings on a female's breast because they signal fertility, availability or whatever. All these answers are equally valid, equally true at the same time. They are not competing. It is just your choice what level of distance you find interesting for your particular question.

Normally, we think that life and behaviour are the result of the environment OR of our genes, nature OR nurture, society OR biology. Moreover, we think that things caused by the environment are easily changed, and thing determined by our genes are, well, determined, and cannot be changed. This is why many people leaning to the progressive, left side of political scale are usually "environmentalists" and many people leaning to the conservative right side of the scale are gene-ist.

Of course, and I won't be surprising you here, things are not that simple, not that black and white (they rarely are in our insanely complicated world). Nature and nurture are intertwined so thoroughly that you cannot tell them apart, unless in very special cases, where one or a few genes, of lack of those genes, have a very specific result. An example of this is Huntington's disease for instance. But let's take a bigger example. Language for instance. Surely, the ability to use language is a unique human ability, enabled somewhere in our genes. This is Nature. But any baby can learn any language in the world as its mother tongue. This is Nurture. So, what is Language? Nature or Nurture? I hope you agree that is a nonsensical question. It is both. Even if we could identify all our "language genes", whatever that means, you still cannot answer that question. Be very suspicious when you read that "a gene for such and so has been discovered". For instance, it might be very possible that some people have a gene or some genes that makes them more likely to be alcoholics. Maybe these genes have built their brain in such a way that alcohol feel really good to them. Or maybe they lack genes that make them hate hangovers. Or maybe...who knows? If these people would grow up in a country where there is no alcohol available, it is very unlikely they would become alcoholics. Nature Nurture? Think twice.

But there is a special way to look at genes and *differences* between people, and this is called behavioural genetics. Let's have a look at this.

Behavioural genetics

We and the things we do are the result of a pretty much infinitely complex interaction of genes and environment, nature and nurture, that is almost impossible to disentangle. But research psychologists are very creative and cunning people, and they have an impressive toolbox of statistics. Maybe we cannot determine the influence of genes and environment in one person, but we can do this for the *variation within a group of people*. We can estimate the percentage of the variation of a certain trait (say length, or IQ) within a group of people that is determined by genes or the environment. To say this differently, we cannot tell how much of your length or IQ is caused by your genes. But we can tell how much of the differences in length or IQ within a group of people is caused by genes. This kind of study focusing on psychological traits is called behavioural genetics. Researchers use the fact that we know how much of their genes identical twins share (100%), non-identical twins share (50%), and brothers and sisters share (50%).

To get a feel for this, say that the correlation in IQ between identical twins is .80, between non-identical twins it is .60 and between brothers and sisters it is .50. You can see that there probably is a genetical basis for IQ. Behavioural geneticists combine this kind of studies with adoption studies if they can. Studying adopted children, especially identical twins that were adopted into two different families are ideal to estimate the influence of genes on psychological traits, because these two twins share all their genes, and nothing of the specific environment.

To be clear: these studies do not find out which genes cause what, or even how many genes cause what. They just estimate the influence of genes and the environment in groups of people on the *variation* of certain traits. This is called the *heritability*.

So, after decades of study using hundreds of thousands of people what are the results on intelligence and personality? Let's start with personality: the five factors OCEAN. In 2015, Vukasović and Bratko did an overview (meta-analysis) of all the behavioural genetic research available so far and they found that on average, 40% of the differences in personality is caused by genes. Specifically: Neuroticism 37%, Extraversion.36%, Openness 41%, Agreeableness .35% and Conscientiousness .31%. These percentages are the same for men and women. For General Intelligence it is even higher: in overview study by Deary and his colleagues estimate that in adults in western societies between 50% to 70% of the differences in intelligence is genetic.

These numbers, paradoxically, indicate that western society is doing a decent job already to help people realise their potential. To understand this, realise that if we could provide an environment to people where everyone would reach their full potential, all what is left in differences between people would be 100% genetic. We seem to be pushing the limits already.

Let's broaden our perspective and go to politics.

References

Deary IJ, Johnson W, Houlihan LM. (2009) Genetic foundations of human intelligence. *Human Genetics*, 126, 215–232

Vukasović, T., & Bratko, D. (2015). Heritability of personality: A meta-analysis of behavior genetic studies. *Psychological Bulletin*, 141, 769-785.

The psychology of the political left and right

Let's first define left, right and liberal for the purposes of this book. The political left is more concerned with social justice and the division of wealth, while the right is more concerned with the production of wealth by individuals. This means that the left is more willing to work with laws and rules, while the right prefers self-regulation by competition. This makes the left progressive, concerned with changing society, while the right is more conservative. The left and the right differ on how much inequality is accepted, and how much social change is seen as desirable. Lately, this political spectrum has considerably polarised, to the degree that people discriminate more on political preference (partisanship) than the classical nationality, gender, or race discrimination. More and more, people from the left and the right do not share any common ground or any common language (what the right calls "duty", the left calls "solidarity", progress is less inequality in society for the Left, and technological innovation for the Right, for example). This will have disastrous consequences, because no matter what, we need to work together or resolve to violence and suppression.

Both the left and the right have a problem with social ethics, psychological reality and economic reality. The problem of the right, favouring a free-market system is that under this system all wealth tends to end up with a few individuals. You only have to think about a game of Monopoly to see how this happens: one player ends up with all the money, which winners will attribute to the wise decisions they made, but actually is purely luck. This tendency to attribute your success to your own skills and your failures to bad luck, while you do exactly the opposite when it concerns others is a basic psychological law. This is called the Fundamental Attribution Error. It is the same with successes in a purely free market economy. Of course, it takes some skill to make it, but many people with the same skills, of even more, end up right at the bottom. The Left is more sensitive to the role of luck in societal success than the Right.

The problem of the left is the complexity of societies and economies. If you reject self-regulation by markets as a system of generating and distributing wealth, you either can rig the system with rules and laws (like anti-trust and monopoly laws for instance) or just directly redistribute and take wealth directly from the top by special taxes, the most logical and efficient way. However, this last measure is usually not easy to implement for two psychological reasons: the wealthy people at the top see their wealth as rightly deserved because of the fundamental attribution error, forgetting all the luck and common infrastructure like transport, juridical, financial system, scientific and technological knowledge that made their wealth possible in the first place. People at the top of the wealth pyramid also tend to be high on conscientiousness (there are far more well-off lawyers than musicians for instance), and as we have seen, conscientious people are far more likely to vote for conservative right-wing politics, abhorring rules and taxes. Thirdly, redistribution is not in their self-interest of course.

This means that simple and efficient redistribution of wealth by taxation is seldom a real option in a democracy (and only a theoretical option in a dictatorship, most dictators seem to be very fond of wealth themselves). What is left is the tedious rigging of the system, making the free market less free to stop all the wealth ending up at the top. Maybe the best general solution would be to make it easy to get rich, but hard to stay rich. One way of doing this is to oblige people to make more and more risky investments of their capital at different levels of wealth. For instance, up to a certain level of wealth you can draw interest, on the next level you can invest in secure stocks and bonds, the next level in less secure options etc.

(I have no idea if this idea has been already explored by policy makers and economists, I could not find anything on Google, and I am not an economist after all. It also falls outside the scope of this book).)My point was: if you reject the free market, you need to come up with plans and you need feedback on these plans. The problem is that the world is so changeable and complex that plans based on an ideology have a very small chance of being effective (can you plan your life five years ahead perfectly?) and that feedback is never on time, and usually very costly in terms of human suffering. Because there is no market economy that tests and corrects, the danger for the left is to end up as totalitarian states. The 20th century has shown us hundreds of millions of deaths by the communism of Stalin and Mao, to name just two big ones.

Yet another problem for the left is that competition and hierarchies are part of human nature. A competitive market economy feels fair (even if it is not), and people tend to work harder for their own profits as for the common good. In every non-market economy, productivity plummets.

Competition requires something to compete about of course, but more interestingly, differences in the ability to compete for something. For instance, if every marathon runner would have exactly the same ability and chance to win, there would be no competition. There would be no match, it would just be a gamble, and it would not be interesting to watch or to enter it as a competitor. You might as well throw a coin. The surprising conclusion is that competition and freedom require differences, inequalities. What inequalities we find acceptable is a choice. To go back to the marathon runners: if we could determine the chances of each runner the win and handicap them accordingly by making them run a larger distance, or giving them a weight to carry or whatever, we again kill the game. Neither do we want to handicap randomly, or even worse, systematically. If we let all people with blue eyes walk with weights, there is no game either. Or to put it in gender differences, when we handicap all men so that women have a chance as well, we do not have a match. Worse still, if we put in the rules that at least fifty per cent of the winners must be women, we also kill the match.

Freedom implies the expression of inequality. Not only inequality of outcome, but even inequality of chances. In the case of a marathon we are willing to accept inequalities in motivation, physical ability and to some extent social inequality. The same choice needs to be made in the way we distribute wealth. People are not equally equipped to compete successfully with others. We will try to correct this by measures and laws: the left wants to do this far more than the right. But enforcing equality of outcome, like putting quota, is destroying freedom itself, with

Left-wing	Right-wing
Slovenly, ambiguous, indifferent	Definite, persistent, tenacious
Eccentric, sensitive, individualistic	Tough, masculine, firm
Open, tolerant, flexible	Reliable, trustworthy, faithful, loyal
Life-loving, free, unpredictable	Stable, consistent
Creative, imaginative, curious	Rigid, intolerant
Expressive, enthusiastic	Conventional, ordinary
Excited, sensation-seeking	Obedient, conformist
Desire for novelty, diversity	Fearful, threatened

potentially terrifying results. And to make the even the discussion of differences between (groups of) people taboo is even more dangerous, because it deprives us of the sorely needed freedom of speech that keeps our democracies alive.

The solution that Western democracies have worked out is walking a path somewhere in the middle by making constant compromises. However, and I come back to this point: This requires an absolute free exchange and debate of ideas, and this in turn requires absolute freedom speech.

Big Five and political preferences

In numerous studies of the last three decades the picture of personality and political preference in terms of left and right (or in the US liberal and conservative) is clear. This was taken from a review of decades of research by Carney and colleagues from 2008.

Uncontrolled, impulsive

Complex, nuanced

Open-minded

Open to experience

Xenophobic, prejudiced

Orderly, organized

Parsimonious, thrifty, stingy

Clean, sterile

Obstinate, stubborn

Aggressive, angry, vengeful

Careful, practical, methodical

Withdrawn, reserved

Stern, cold, mechanical

Anxious, suspicious, obsessive

Self-controlled

Restrained, inhibited

Concerned with rules, norms

Moralistic

Simple, decisive

Closed-minded

Conscientious

The picture is crystal clear: the two most relevant personality dimensions determining political preferences are Openness and Conscientiousness. People high on Openness tend to be left-wing, people high on Conscientiousness tend to be more right-wing.

The same, accidently, occurs in organisations. The larger an organisation becomes, the more regulated it becomes, and the better people high on conscientiousness function in it, are attracted to it and hired. Consciousness is a good predictor of job success in most jobs, (but not all). The trouble is, people and organisations that value conscientiousness, tend to dislike people high on

Openness. But people on Openness are the ones with original crazy ideas and motivations are the innovators, and the ones who can adapt an organisation when the environment and market changes. This may be one of the main reasons why large companies seldom survive longer than a few decades at most. A company run by people high on Openness is like a ship on erratic course with no goal, a company run by people high on Conscientiousness is like a ship that cannot change course until it is too late, and it hits the rocks. This is perfectly illustrated in the classic BBC series "Yes Minister", where the Head of the Civil Service Sir Humphrey has the following discussion with his minister Hacker:

Sir Humphrey: My job is to carry out government policy.
Hacker: Even if you think it's wrong?
Sir Humphrey: Well, almost all government policy is
wrong, but... frightfully well carried out.

And because personality traits are relatively stable (they appear at a very early age too), political preference is stable too. All that is left is talking together and compromise. And this brings us to free speech again.

References
Carney, D.R, John T., Jost, J.T., Samuel D., Gosling, S.D., and Potter, J. (2008). The Secret Lives of Liberals

and Conservatives: Personality Profiles, Interaction Styles, and the Things They Leave Behind. *Political Psychology*, 29, 807-840

Ekstrom, P. D. and Federico, C. M. (2018), Personality and Political Preferences Over Time: Evidence From a Multi-Wave Longitudinal Study. *Journal of Personality*. Accepted Author Manuscript.

Gerber, A.S., Huber, G.A., Doherty, D. et al. (2012) Personality and the Strength and Direction of Partisan Identification. *Political Behavior*, 34, 653-688

Free speech

Free speech is under attack. Let's first look at some scary results from a recent study. A Cato Institute survey of 3,000 Americans with university experience found that 40 percent would ban speakers who say men on average are better than women at math, 49 percent would ban speakers who criticise the police, 41 percent would ban speakers who say undocumented immigrants should be deported, 74 percent said universities should ban speakers if students threaten violent protest, 51 percent said it was OK to prevent others from hearing a speaker.

It is easy to see how these attitudes flow directly from post-modern thinking, where language is not seen as a means, but as weapon of repression, and equality is the goal of everything. These results are scary, to say the least, because freedom of speech is the most fundamental mechanism we have to maintain our system of self-government by democracy. This follows directly from the fact that we need speech, concepts and ideas to think and form opinions. If you take away this freedom of exchange of ideas, even contemplation of ideas becomes impossible (because the ideas themselves do not exist anymore). This is of course worked out most brilliantly by George Orwell in this terrifying book "1984", where ideas are systematically erased and there is no more connection between reality and thought.

"Not merely the validity of experience, but the very existence of external reality was tacitly denied by their philosophy…. "Don't you see that the whole aim of Newspeak is to narrow the range of thought? In the end we shall make thoughtcrime literally impossible, because there will be no words in which to express it."

The problem of any system of government is: who is controlling it. I cannot resist this most famous Latin quote here, sorry: *Quis custodiet ipsos custodes?* who guards the guards themselves? In a democracy the answer to this is: we all do. As the philosopher of freedom of speech Meiklejohn noted (ironically in the 1948, when Orwell wrote his 1984), in a free government, people do not speak of favours, but of rights. They do not bargain, but they reason. That makes democracy very messy, and we are obviously still struggling to get to grips with the precise way of using and maintaining it.

In any case, to be able to reason, and to self-govern, to vote, voters need to have access to all relevant ideas and information, not just the ones that they, or even worse, one group of people, happen to agree with. In fact, it is precisely the essence of the democratic process to discuss, to have access to alien ideas, so we can make informed decisions, and correct mistakes. To be able to vote, people need access to ALL ideas and concepts, before they can make an informed decision. All facts, all interests must be considered before a wise decision about consequent actions can be made. Without conflicting ideas, there is no discussion, and no democracy. When you censor ideas because a minority or a majority regards them as false or dangerous, you kill our ability to self-govern. This means that goal of freedom of speech is not the expression of ideas for its own sake, but to get these ideas into the minds of others, so we can make informed decisions. If you start manipulating the process of free speech, you kill democracy. Democracy is closely related to the concept of a "Market Place of Ideas" where ideas compete for truth and utility.

So, what are the limits of free speech? In a democracy, this question gets us into a catch 22 situation: we must decide for ourselves, by using …. free speech. It may be clear that limiting this "meta-free speech", free speech about free speech is extremely dangerous. This is where dictatorship begins (and ends). We need to be careful with concepts like "Hate Speech". Most commonly, Hate Speech is only recognized as such when it poses a *clear* AND *imminent*, pressing danger to other people, but the interpretation of this is being stretched more and more. Moreover, the limits of free speech should be enforced after, and not before expression or publication. We correct wrongs by our judicial systems after the facts, we do not censor before. Or at least, we should.

Being offensive is certainly not a reason for censorship. Nearly all ideas can be seen offensive to someone. What is offensive is different in different times and different places. For instance, not so long ago it was considered offensive to give public speeches about gay rights, now it would be offensive to give a speech against gay rights. What changed? Well, for one thing, the application of the right of free speech to talk about gay rights when this was considered offensive. It is important to realise that nothing has changed about the importance about this principle. We are not "right" now, like we are not "right" then. The idea that one time or one group of people is in possession of the ultimate truth is the root of the destruction of democracy, and the rise of a totalitarian state. And this has never ended well.

References

Ceci, S. J., & Williams, W.M. (2018). Who Decides What Is Acceptable Speech on Campus? Why Restricting Free Speech Is Not the Answer. Perspectives on Psychological Science, *13*, 299–323.

http://journals.sagepub.com/doi/full/10.1177/17456916
18767324

Meiklejohn, Alexander (1948). *Free speech and its relation to self-government*. New York: Harper.

Mill, J.S. (1859). *On Liberty*. http://www.feedbooks.com/book/4202

Putting it all together

Gender seems to be, for better or for worse, one of the most prominent issues on the political agenda. The aim of this book was to give you a short overview of the scientific psychological knowledge and the ideological backgrounds to be able to make up your own mind about gender politics. The scientific literature shows beyond any doubt that women score higher on verbal intelligence, men score higher on spatial intelligence and mathematic skills. Regarding personality, women score higher on agreeableness and neuroticism, and men score higher on openness to new experiences. Men are more aggressive, competitive and ambitious. These robust systematic psychological differences make sense in the light of our evolutionary past, especially the process of sexual selection: female choice, male competition. Research into the genetical base of personality and intelligence has shown that there is a considerable genetic influence, highest for intelligence, and substantial for personality.

These differences have large consequences in highly selective environments, because of tail effects (the fact that at the tail of the normal distribution the proportion of men and women gets more and more skewed), where one gender can outnumber the other considerably even when gender differences are relatively small.

Personality differences are also relevant to political preferences and ideologies. Right-wing voters score high on Conscientiousness, while left-wing voters score high on Openness. These differences are again stable. Both a purely right-wing system and a left-wing system will end in gross social injustice: a right-wing system will end up with the accumulation of wealth with very few people while the rest of the population is starving, while a purely left-wing system will end up in totalitarian states. The best hope for a fair society is continuous compromise by means of discussion, which requires absolute free speech.

Scientific facts are largely ignored by current gender politics. This has two reasons: the Left maintains that all differences between men and women are caused by differential treatment of men and women by society. It this view, gender differences are easily fixed by simply reforming society. However, the dominant ideology of gender politics is post-modernism and this ideology takes this idea a step further. According to post-modernist thinking, free speech, like all language, has no basis at all. It is simply an instrument of power by the dominant group of people (in this case white heterosexual males). In this view, everything is subjected to on goal: absolute equality, and anything that may contradict or question this ideal is per definition wrong and must be supressed. The Social Warrior Movement is an obvious exponent of post-modern ideology.

The gravest danger of gender politics and post-modern thinking is ignoring inconvenient scientific facts, but above all the insistence on the destruction of free speech. Free speech is the correction mechanism of individuals: we learn what we do not know by acquiring ideas in the form of language of others. Free speech is also the correction mechanism of democracies, keeping us on the middle path between the extremes of left-wing and right- wing hell.